J 973.43 SCH

D1156312

early challenge
t

Life in the New American Nation™

The Whiskey Rebellion

An Early Challenge to America's New Government

Katy Schiel

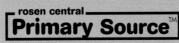

rosen central
Primary Source™

The Rosen Publishing Group Inc., New York

For my fourth-grade teacher, Evelyn Bejcek, who always made learning so much fun

Published in 2004 by The Rosen Publishing Group, Inc.
29 East 21st Street, New York, NY 10010

Copyright © 2004 by The Rosen Publishing Group, Inc.

First Edition

All rights reserved. No part of this book may be reproduced in any form without permission in writing from the publisher, except by a reviewer.

Library of Congress Cataloging-in-Publication Data

Schiel, Katy.
The Whiskey Rebellion : an early challenge to America's new government/ by Katy Schiel.— 1st ed.
    p. cm. — (Life in the new American nation)
Summary: Discusses the first challenge to the new federal government of the United States, which began in 1794 when citizens of western Pennsylvania took up arms to fight against a new federal excise tax on whiskey.
Includes bibliographical references and index.
ISBN 0-8239-4044-6 (lib. bdg.)
ISBN 0-8239-4262-7 (pbk. bdg.)
6-pack ISBN 0-8239-4263-5
1. Whiskey Rebellion, Pa., 1794—Juvenile literature. [1. Whiskey Rebellion, Pa., 1794. 2. Frontier and pioneer life—Pennsylvania. 3. Pennsylvania—History—1775–1865.] I. Title. II. Series.
E315 .S35 2004
973.4'3—dc21

2002152883

Manufactured in the United States of America

Cover left side: Engraving of General Daniel Morgan
Cover right side: Secret Whisky Still in the Mountains

Photo credits: cover photos (left and right), pp. 1, 6 © Corbis; pp. 8, 13, 16, 19 © Library of Congress; pp. 10, 23, 25, 26 © Hulton/Archive/Getty Images; p. 14 © National Archives and Records Administration.

Designer and Photo Researcher: Nelson Sá; Editor: Eliza Berkowitz

Contents

Introduction

On July 16, 1794, fifty angry men carrying rifles marched to the home of General John Neville. Neville lived in Bower Hill in western Pennsylvania. The men demanded that Neville surrender to them. A fight broke out between the men and Neville's supporters. As the fight raged, Neville's house was burned down and three men were killed. What could have caused this fight? General Neville was a Revolutionary War hero. He had been a very popular man in the area. But once he became the tax collector for the new federal excise tax on whiskey, he made enemies.

The farmers in the area hated this tax. They also hated all of the people who tried to collect it. The event at Bower Hill was the first battle of the Whiskey Rebellion. The Whiskey Rebellion was the first challenge to the new federal government of the United States of America.

The Stirrings of Rebellion   Chapter 1

In the 1700s, western Pennsylvania was a very quiet area. It was separated from Philadelphia by five hundred miles of wilderness and mountains. During this time, Philadelphia was the seat of the federal government. To the west was America's frontier, an area that was still unsettled. The people who lived there were very independent. Most of them were farmers. People worked very hard to survive and to feed their families. Native Americans were angry with the frontier people for taking their land. The Native Americans attacked the frontier people constantly.

In the 1790s, America was a new country. The idea of a strong central government was a new

In this illustration, three men who are making whiskey are being warned that police officers are on their way. During the Whiskey Rebellion, officers collected taxes on whiskey, much to the dismay of those making it.

idea. Today we live in a country that has a strong central government. The federal government has more power than individual states. But right after America gained its independence from England, people were still arguing about this. In the eastern states, such as Massachusetts and New York, people wanted a strong central government. In the independent West, however, they did not.

The settlers of western Pennsylvania did not like the idea of a distant government. They wanted their own government to control their own affairs. Before the Revolutionary War in 1775, they even wished to break away from Pennsylvania. They wanted to name their colony Westsylvania. After America won its independence,

What is this stuff called whiskey over which everyone was fighting? Whiskey is basically just grains and water that is turned into a type of liquor. The grain is ground up into a product called grist. The grist is then mixed with water and cooked, fermented (allowed to get really, really old!), then distilled (cleaned up). When it gets to this point, it becomes very strong. The word "whiskey" comes from the Gaelic word *uisgebaugh*, which is translated as "water of life."

they felt strongly that the U.S. Constitution promised a strong state government. They thought it was unfair for their land to be controlled by a power that was five hundred miles away. In those days, when transportation was slower, five hundred miles was very far to go.

Whiskey was very important to the frontier people. It was more than just a drink to them. Roads were

In the late 1700s, whiskey was very valuable. This illustration, which was originally published in *Frank Leslie's Illustrated Newspaper*, is an unflattering portrait of Native Americans attempting to drink whiskey that has been spilled by the authorities.

bad, and transporting extra grain to sell was difficult. So farmers made whiskey from their extra grain. Twenty-four bushels of grain would make sixteen gallons of whiskey. Transporting the smaller amounts of liquor was much easier. Every autumn, the western farmers brought the whiskey to other areas. They could trade the whiskey for things that they needed, such as iron and salt. Whiskey often took the place of money. It was very valuable.

As America grew, settlers pushed farther into the lands where the Native Americans had lived for thousands of years. Naturally, the Native American people were very angry about this. They wanted the settlers to leave. Fights between the two peoples occurred all the time.

Often, the Native Americans were led by the British, who were also enemies of young America. In the 1700s, thousands of settlers were attacked and killed by Native Americans. In return, the settlers would attack and kill many Native Americans, even if they were peaceful. These fights were called the Indian Wars.

This illustration was originally published in *Harper's Magazine* in February 1888. The artist, Howard Pyle, depicts a group of American soldiers finding one of their own murdered by Native Americans. In the 1700s, it was not uncommon for Native Americans and American soldiers to attack one another.

The young country could not overlook this terrible problem. The government sent groups of people to fight the Native Americans in 1790 and again in 1791. Both times the government troops were defeated. To raise money, Alexander Hamilton proposed that Congress tax the whiskey produced in the western frontier.

Chapter 2 — The Troubles Begin

Alexander Hamilton was the secretary of the treasury. He was a very strong believer in a powerful federal government. He thought that the states should have very little power. He also thought that the U.S. government should be led by wealthy landowners. He believed that working people should have very little input into how the country was run. It was Hamilton's idea to tax the whiskey. Taxing the poor farmers would be easy, he thought, because they had no power. He was wrong.

After much arguing, Congress approved the excise tax on whiskey in 1790. This tax was imposed on all of the frontier areas, not just

This painting of Alexander Hamilton was created by John Trumball in 1792. Hamilton was secretary of the treasury from 1789 to 1795. Many people were outraged by his idea to tax whiskey. Debates occurred over whether or not the tax was fair.

western Pennsylvania. The frontier people were very upset about the new tax. Many signed petitions to have the tax dropped. Why was this tax so horrible to the people in western Pennsylvania? The biggest

Many tax collectors were attacked when they visited farmers to collect the tax on whiskey. In this image, a group of people are tarring and feathering a government inspector. To tar and feather someone means to coat someone with a layer of tar and then a layer of feathers.

reason was money. The tax was collected where the whiskey was made, not where it was sold. This meant that the farmers were not only being taxed on whiskey they sold but also on whiskey they drank! They believed that this was very unfair. They were poor people, and whiskey was one of their few luxuries in life. Plus, they felt that they did not benefit from the new tax. Why should they pay their hard-earned money to some distant government?

To register for the tax, the farmers had to travel long distances. The government knew how independent the western people were, and they knew that the people of Washington County, Pennsylvania, were especially independent. The government was afraid that the tax offices would be burned down if they were set up in the settlements. For this reason, they put tax-collecting offices far from where the farmers lived. If a farmer resisted the tax, as many did, they had to go on trial. The only courthouse was in Philadelphia, more than five hundred miles away. To get there, a farmer had to leave his crops, sometimes during the middle of the harvest season. It was

CALIFORNIA,
Washington County Pennsylvania
1902

This panoramic map, drawn by Thaddeus Mortimer Fowler in 1902, shows the city of California in Washington County, Pennsylvania. Residents of this area were upset with the tax on whiskey and rebelled against the tax and anyone who tried to collect it.

terribly difficult to do this because the profits from the crops were needed for the families to live.

All in all, the people in Washington County were fed up with the way they were being treated by the federal government. They decided to fight back. At first, the farmers protested peacefully. A group of men met at Redstone Fort in Brownsville, Pennsylvania.

They thought that if they argued their case well, the government would listen. It did not work. Then came protests in which the settlers used force. Once in a while, a tax collector would come to Washington County to try to do his job, but the farmers would not allow him to carry on his business. A few times, groups of farmers captured a tax collector. They dipped him in tar, covered him with feathers, and then paraded him around the streets while the townspeople made fun of him!

Chapter 3 The Federal Government's Show of Strength

In July 1794, the real protests started. On July 15, General John Neville began to hand out summonses to Pennsylvania farmers. Most of them had never paid the whiskey tax, but now the government wanted them to pay. The summonses told them to stop working and go to Philadelphia right away to be tried in court. This was during the busy harvest season, and the farmers needed to work. If this was not bad enough, terrible rumors began to spread. The rumor was that if the farmers did not go to Philadelphia, they would be dragged away by force. This made the farmers scared and angry.

The next morning at dawn, a group of angry men marched to John Neville's house in Bower Hill. Neville ordered them to stay back. Then he fired his gun into the crowd, killing one man. The angry mob left but returned the next day with men from the militia. A militia is a group of regular people who have organized themselves into an army. The commander of the militia was James McFarlane. As was Neville, McFarlane was a Revolutionary War hero. But McFarlane supported the farmers. He ordered Neville to surrender. He also ordered the ten soldiers guarding

Luckily, one of John Neville's houses, called Woodville, remains to this day and is now a national historical landmark. His other house in Bower Hill was burned down during the Whiskey Rebellion.

James McFarlane's
Final Resting Place

If you go to the Mingo Presbyterian Church in Washington County, Pennsylvania, today, you can see the final resting place of James McFarlane. His headstone explains how he fought for American independence. It also speaks of his accomplishments and untimely death. In short, it explains that he was a courageous and well-respected man who died fighting for his rights. Many people grieved for him.

Neville's house to leave. They refused, and shots broke out. During the confusion, McFarlane thought the fighting had stopped. He stepped out from the tree he was hiding behind. A shower of bullets broke out and killed him. The mob became very angry. The men set fire to Neville's house, the finest one in the neighborhood, and burned it to the ground. All in all, three people were killed and several were hurt.

One of the leaders of the group was a young lawyer named David Bradford. Bradford spoke strongly against the whiskey tax and vowed to destroy it. He called a meeting of rebels for August 1. More than five thousand men showed up. Bradford led the men to Pittsburgh, Pennsylvania. The leaders talked boldly about independence and civil war. They wanted to burn Pittsburgh, the seat of the much-hated local government, but they were not well organized. Pittsburgh did not get burned down that day. In fact, the local people were very nice to the rebels and even gave them food to eat and whiskey to drink! Overall, the rebels were fairly harmless. They were very angry about the whiskey tax, but they were not a serious danger to the federal government. The government, however, did not see it that way.

President George Washington was very angry. He called an emergency meeting. He wanted to protect the United States against further revolts. Alexander Hamilton believed that force would be necessary to defeat the rebels. So, on August 7, 1794, President Washington got about 13,000 troops together. He also sent three commissioners to western Pennsylvania to try and solve the problems without resorting to force.

In late August, the three commissioners met with a committee. The commissioners promised a general pardon to the men if they promised to be peaceful. Many did not want to accept this. They believed that if they went along with the commissioners, they would be admitting guilt. However, after talking about it for a while, they finally accepted the pardon.

Chapter 4   The Aftermath

Although the rebels had agreed to be peaceful, Washington and Hamilton believed that the government had to appear strong. To end the rebellion, the government had to show the rebels who was in control. Even though the rebels agreed to be peaceful, the thirteen thousand troops were called up to fight. Most of these troops were from New Jersey and Maryland. On October 4, the troops came together at Carlisle and Cumberland, Pennsylvania. There, Washington reviewed the troops. It was also there that he heard news from the West. Two representatives told him all was calm. The troops were not needed anymore.

Washington still wanted a show of strength. Finally, on October 24, the federal troops entered Pittsburgh. Federal officials went along with the troops. Their job was to find the leaders of the Whiskey Rebellion. By mid-November, they were searching for the leaders in western Pennsylvania. In the end, eighteen people were arrested, but the real leaders were never found. These men were marched to Philadelphia to stand trial. David Bradford, one of the biggest leaders of the Whiskey Rebellion, escaped south to Louisiana. He was never caught.

This engraving of Henry Lee was done by G. R. Hall around 1800. Lee was commander of the army that assembled to try to stop the Whiskey Rebellion. He is also remembered for his active political career.

23

The Watermelon Army

The federal army had a terrible journey to western Pennsylvania. It was hard to get important supplies to the troops. More than half became sick with dysentery. The trip was slow because they had to stop and rest many times. All in all, it was a very sad army! This army of 13,000 troops is now called the watermelon army. This is because one of the rebels, James Bracken-ridge, wrote a funny song about them. It went: "Brothers, you may not think to frighten us . . . [with] water-melon armies from the Jersey shores; they would cut a much better figure in warring with the crabs and oysters about the Capes of Delaware."

Back in Philadelphia, the eighteen men were charged with treason. Their lawyers argued that they were involved in the riots but were not the leaders of them. After a long trial, sixteen of the men were set free. President Washington pardoned the other two.

The Whiskey Rebellion was now finished. Luckily, only a few people had died in it. The rebels did not get their wish to have the whiskey tax done away with, but farmers in western Pennsylvania still did not pay their taxes. So who won? Alexander Hamilton thought that the federal government had won. This was because the argument showed how powerful the government was. Indeed, President Washington proved that the federal government would use force to stop any rebellion against it, but, in a way, the rebels won. This is because they succeeded in not paying the tax. The biggest result of the Whiskey Rebellion was political. Right after the conflict, Hamilton's Federalist Party won control of Congress, but that victory was short-lived. In 1795, a major figure in the Whiskey Rebellion, Albert Gallatin, an Anti-Federalist, was elected to the House of Representatives. Albert Gallatin's election proved that his party was gaining strength.

Albert Gallatin, pictured here circa 1840, was a part of the Anti-Federalist political party. After the Whiskey Rebellion ended, Gallatin was elected to the House of Representatives. His political party gained strength.

The only real victim of the Whiskey Rebellion, besides the men who died, was Secretary of State Edmund Randolph. Randolph was President Washington's closest and most trusted adviser and friend. In August 1795, one year after the Whiskey Rebellion, Randolph was accused of treason. Two

In 1795, a year after the end of the Whiskey Rebellion, Secretary of State Edmund Randolph was accused of starting the rebellion for political gain. He was a part of George Washington's first presidential cabinet, pictured here in 1788. Randolph returned to his law practice and counseled Aaron Burr when Burr was tried for treason in 1807.

members of Washington's cabinet, Timothy Pickering and Oliver Wolcott, told President Washington that they had a letter. This letter said that Edmund Randolph and the Federalists had actually started the Whiskey Rebellion for political gain. Randolph swore that he did nothing wrong and that he could prove it. He knew that Pickering and Wolcott were lying, but it was too late. Washington had lost trust in his old friend, and Randolph's career was finished. This shows how bitter politics were in the years after the Whiskey Rebellion.

It was not until 1802 that the excise tax on whiskey was finally abolished. The first challenge to the federal government of the United States was truly finished.

The Great Escape

As David Bradford sat at home on October 24, he was warned that a cavalry unit was coming to arrest him. According to popular legend, he leapt from the second-story window of the house right onto a waiting horse. From there he made it to the Ohio River, where he met a sympathetic skipper on a boat. After a series of close calls, Bradford and the skipper finally made it to the safety of New Orleans.

Glossary

abolish (uh-BAH-lish) To do away with.

adviser (ad-VYZ-ur) A person who gives advice or guidance.

commissioner (kuh-MIH-shun-ur) A person authorized by a commission to perform certain duties.

dysentery (DIH-sun-ter-ee) A sickness of the intestines accompanied by diarrhea.

excise tax (EK-syz TAKS) A tax that the government puts on a product that is produced, sold, or consumed in its own country.

federal government (FEH-duh-rul GUH-vern-mint) The central government of a country.

frontier (frun-TEER) The edge of a settled country, where the wilderness begins.

liquor (LIH-kur) A distilled alcoholic drink.

marshal (MAR-shul) An officer of various kinds.

militia (muh-LIH-shuh) A military force composed of ordinary citizens, not professional soldiers.

petition (puh-TIH-shun) A formal way to ask for something to be done.

rebel (REH-bul) A person who fights against government or authority.

rebellion (ruh-BEL-yun) A fight against one's government.

revolt (rih-VOLT) To fight or rebel.

rumor (ROO-mur) A story that is heard by people with no proof that it's true.

surrender (suh-REN-dur) To give up.

treason (TREE-zun) A betrayal of trust or confidence; a betrayal of one's country by helping its enemies.

Web Sites

Due to the changing nature of Internet links, the Rosen Publishing Group, Inc., has developed an online list of Web sites related to the subject of this book. This site is updated regularly. Please use this link to access the list:

http://www.rosenlinks.com/lnan/whre

Primary Source Image List

Page 8: Photographic print, published in *Frank Leslie's Illustrated Newspaper* on February 3, 1872. Housed in the Denver Public Library.
Page 10: The illustration, "On the Outposts–1780," by Howard Pyle, originally published in *Harper's Magazine* in February 1888.
Page 13: Painting by John Trumball. Created in 1792.
Page 14: Drawing by D. C. Johnson. Housed in the National Archives and Records Administration.
Page 16: Panoramic map, drawn by Thaddeus Mortimer Fowler in 1902.
Page 19: Photograph from 1997. Housed in the Pittsburgh History & Landmarks Foundation in Pennsylvania.
Page 23: Engraving by G. R. Hall. Housed in the National Archives and Records Administration.
Page 25: Painting by Alonzo Chappel. Housed in the National Archives and Records Administration.

Index

About the Author

Katy Schiel is a writer and former bicycle messenger who lives near Boston with her husband and two cats.